Speaking in TONGUES

Your Secret Weapon

TODD SMITH

SPEAKING IN TONGUES
by Todd Smith
Copyright © 2019 Todd Smith

ISBN: 9781691410965

Cover Design: Marty Darracott

Dedication

It is with great love that I dedicate this book to the North Georgia Revival pastors who have labored arm–and-arm with me, my staff, my church and each other. Together we have had the privilege to host the precious presence of God.

You have graciously demonstrated, at the highest level, Biblical humility. I have watched each of you prefer your brother over yourself. You have loved and honored one another, and I am confident this has made our Father happy.

Your preaching has penetrated the deepest realm of darkness. Your revelation and passion for the heart of God is remarkable. With grace you communicate His love to all. You have boldly and gently prepared the way for people to find God as you encouraged them all to meet Him in the water.

I am forever grateful to each of you.

Todd

Introduction

The book of Acts fearlessly unveils God's plan for His Church. Each chapter is a real life drama that displays two kingdoms in brutal conflict. It reveals how the body of Christ could and should walk as it advances the Kingdom of God. It is a Church of demonstration and transformation.

It started with Jesus' miraculous ascension and escalated quickly to a top floor stuffed full of His desperate followers.

On the tenth day, the promise of the Father came, the entire room was filled with God's glory, and 120 of Jesus' disciples spoke in tongues. All of them. Not one of them was left out or didn't receive this blessing.

If the Church was birthed with this demonstration of fire, it stands to reason that it should continue in it. This book is written to help each of us understand the value of speaking in tongues. Make no mistake about it; God's will is for you to realize there is more, and that tongues is your secret weapon.

Table of Contents

Chapter One

THE NEW YORK TIMES and TONGUES

It is a wonderful occasion when medical science supports and affirms what the Bible has to say. As we all know, these moments can be somewhat rare. However, what may be more fascinating is when the *New York Times* reports the extraordinary news in a positive fashion.

On November 7, 2006, the *New York Times* reported on the valuable research done by Dr. Andrew Newberg on speaking in tongues (a thorough review of his research is in chapter two). In addition to reviewing Dr. Newberg's study, the *New York Times* referenced another study that was conducted on 1,000 evangelical Christians in England. Here is what they reported:

"Contrary to what may be a common perception, studies suggest that people who speak in tongues rarely suffer from mental problems. A recent study of nearly 1,000 evangelical Christians in England found that those who engaged in the practice were more emotionally stable than those who did not."[1]

Don't miss what was reported. It is significant and revelatory.

It must be stated again. Benedict Carey who wrote the article included this statement:

"...people who speak in tongues rarely suffer from mental problems...and were more emotionally stable than those who did not."
New York Times, 2006

Wow! This is captivating at all levels. This revelation is monumental and has enormous ramifications for the people of God who pray in tongues. This alone should pique our interest and cause us to pray in the Spirit more.

Think about the impact that speaking in tongues can have on you, both spiritually and physically.

---

[1] *New York Times*
https://www.nytimes.com/2006/11/07/health/07brain.html

Now, apply that to your loved ones. I know you want them to experience all that God has for them.

This report is not a preacher telling you the spiritual and physical advantages. But it is the *New York Times* revealing a study that praying in tongues helps your mental health.

It is a fact that too many people, even Charismatics and Pentecostals, undervalue speaking in tongues. Perhaps they don't see that it is necessary. Sadly, they have adopted that mindset because not enough pastors and church leaders are emphasizing praying in tongues to the degree they should.

God never intended for us to place this blessed privilege on the back burner. No, it has to be front and center in our lives as well as our churches.

Prepare yourself, because God is about to take you to a new level in your walk with Him. Moving forward, you will no longer live below God's intentional best for your life.

Chapter Two

A UNIVERSITY STUDY SUPPORTS BIBLE EXPLANATION OF SPEAKING IN TONGUES

The Neuroscience Department in the medical school at the University of Pennsylvania conducted a provocative study on speaking in tongues and the affect it has on the brain.

The doctor overseeing the study was Dr. Andrew Newberg, Associate Professor in the Department of Radiology and Psychiatry and Adjunct Professor in the Department of Religious Studies. He is also board certified in Internal Medicine, Nuclear Medicine, and Nuclear Cardiology.

Dr. Newberg said, regarding those subjects who were studied while speaking in tongues, "We noticed a number of changes that occurred functionally in the brain. Our finding of decreased activity in the frontal lobes during the practice of speaking in tongues is fascinating because these subjects truly believed that the Spirit of God is moving through them and controlling what was being spoken."[2]

For those who don't know, the frontal lobe helps us achieve our day-to-day activities such as thinking, reasoning, planning, managing and controlling emotions. In addition, it aids in making decisions, solving problems and even speaking. Newberg's research revealed that when the participants in his study sang gospel songs in English, the frontal lobes were alert and active, showing the subjects had to think about what they were saying or singing. However, when they sang and spoke in tongues the activity in the frontal lobe was nearly nonexistent.

Dr. Newberg also conducted the same test on a local pastor, finding that "The scan showed that the frontal lobe, the part of the brain that controls language, was active when he prayed in English. But for the most part, fell quiet when he prayed in

---

2

https://discernthetime.wordpress.com/2013/10/04/speakin g-in-tongues-medical-study-proves-its-the-holy-spirit-praying/

tongues."[3]

It is a fact that the frontal lobe activity increases when a person focuses on what they are saying. This finding confirms that when people speak in tongues, the words coming forth originate from a source other than the mind.

In addition, it was revealed that while blood flow to the frontal lobes decreased, activity in the area that controls self awareness was active. This is interesting. This reveals that the subjects knew what was happening around them and that they were not out of "control" or in some kind of mystical trance.

Dr. Newberg says, "Our brain imaging research shows us that these subjects are not in control of the usual language centers during this activity (when praying in tongues)."

He further stated to *ABC News*: "It's not language - it's not regular language, at least, that would normally activate the frontal lobe [of the brain]."[4]

He adds, "These findings could be interpreted as

---

[3] *Christian Post*
https://www.christianpost.com/voice/medical-study-proves-validity-speaking-in-tongues.html
[4] Christian Post,
https://www.christianpost.com/voice/medical-study-proves-validity-speaking-in-tongues.html

the subjects' sense of self being taken over by something else. We, scientifically, assume it's being taken over by another part of the brain, but we couldn't see where it took place."

What does all this mean and what does it substantiate?

First, often it seems that science and the Bible are in conflict with one another. This study goes a long way in affirming the value of praying in tongues.

Second, the study revealed that the frontal lobe of the brain is highly active when we speak and pray in our native language, but the activity of the frontal lobe decreases significantly when we pray in tongues. Thus, certifying what Paul said, *"When I pray in tongues **my spirit prays** but my understanding is unfruitful"* (1 Corinthians 14:5).

The Apostle Paul knew two thousand years ago what this study only recently validated. Praying in tongues comes from your spirit, not your brain.

This is a key point moving forward.

Chapter Three

BOOST YOUR IMMUNE SYSTEM - PRAY IN TONGUES

According to a survey funded by the Bill and Melinda Gates foundation, they found that 95% of the world has a health issue of some kind. The new study revealed that less than 5% of people worldwide had no health problems.[5]

It is staggering to realize in today's health-crazed society that 95% of the people alive are actively dealing with some sort of a health issue.

It is estimated that half of all Americans take

---

[5] Live Science https://www.livescience.com/51122-world-health-problems.html

multivitamins. All told, Americans will spend nearly thirty billion dollars annually on vitamins and herbal supplements.

In the midst of their pursuit of health, people are looking for ways to boost their immune system in order to live healthier lives. Medically, it is a proven fact that a healthy immune system can prevent one from getting sick and/or contracting a disease while helping them live longer.

MILLION DOLLAR QUESTION:

Do you want to improve your health?

I've got something for you - Pray in Tongues.

You read that right: pray in tongues.

I think what follows will excite you and help make you a healthier person.

Carl Peterson, M.D., a brain specialist, conducted a study on the relationship between the brain and speaking in tongues. In part, his study highlighted the physical benefits of praying in tongues. He worked on this study at ORU in Tulsa, Oklahoma.

There are many intriguing facts that surfaced during his study, one of which was when we spend extended times in prayer and/or worship in the Spirit (using our heavenly prayer language), there is an activity that begins to take place in our brain. As we pray in tongues, the brain begins to release two chemical secretions that are directed into our immune systems, giving a thirty-five to forty percent boost to the immune system.[6]

According to Dr. Peterson, "A very significant percentage of the central nervous system is directly and indirectly activated in the process of extended verbal and musical prayer (tongues and singing in tongues) over a period of time. This results in a significant release of brain hormones which, in turn, increases the body's general immunity."[7]

"We do know the part of the brain affected ... [it] represents a significant portion of the brain and its metabolic activity. Therefore, voluntary speech during extended vocal prayer causes a major stimulation in these parts of the brain (mainly the hypothalamus)."[8]

Peterson correctly pinpointed the hypothalamus as the portion of the brain that is greatly impacted by our praying in tongues.

---

[6] Mark Virkler, https://www.cwgministries.org/blogs/health-benefits-speaking-tongues
[7] Dr. Carl Peterson, http://www.thequickenedword.com/rhema/TONGUESSTUDY.HTML
[8] Ibid

He adds, "The hypothalamus has direct regulation of four major portions of the body a) the pituitary gland and all target endocrine glands; b) the total immune system; c) the entire autonomic system; and d) the production of brain hormones called endorphins and enkephalins, which are chemicals that the body produces and are 100-200 times more powerful than morphine."[9]

What is the result? Praying in tongues promotes healing and health in the body. What this study reveals is compelling. Think about the ramifications of us praying in the Spirit for continued periods of time. Not only are we affecting the world, growing and advancing the Kingdom of God through intercession, but, in the midst of it, we are enhancing our health.

Again, according to his research the secretion of chemicals into our system that releases potential healing and builds our immune system is triggered by our time of extended praying in and singing in tongues.

---

[9] Ibid

Chapter Four

SCARED TO DEATH

Can you recall the first time you heard someone speak in tongues? I can. Boy, was I shocked, surprised, confused, and deeply scared! I was at a Pentecostal church in Alabama during a camp meeting night. Because it was "Camp Meeting time," people were already spiritually and emotionally primed. It didn't take much to get them to shout, scream, dance, jump and cry. None of the above was I accustomed to in church.

Then "it" happened. The speaker, out of nowhere, gave the command for the whole bunch to start speaking in tongues. And on cue, everyone around me began to do just that. I didn't have time to prepare for it; it happened so fast. In my mind I thought, "Have you guys lost your minds? Are you crazy? What is this?"

Needless to say, my first encounter wasn't positive at all. I left the meeting with a bad taste in my mouth and assumed incorrectly that what I saw and encountered was extreme emotionalism and, mostly, not of God.

In general, such assumptions seem to be the case with many of us. Why? Perhaps, like me, you were brought up in a denomination that didn't support, practice and, worse yet, didn't even believe in tongues. Therefore, it was always spoken of in a negative way or not spoken of at all. It was taboo. Furthermore, those who "did it" were a little off center, and in my former viewpoint, unstable.

I want to help you have a Biblical understanding of the importance and necessity of tongues. I trust that what I share will answer your questions and lead you into the remarkable blessing of speaking in tongues

Of all the essential doctrines in the Bible, there isn't a more controversial subject than that of tongues. History substantiates that this topic has divided churches, denominations, friends, families and even marriages. What God has meant for a blessing to the whole body of Christ has become a divisive tool of the "haves and have nots."

Jesus didn't give this precious gift to the Church for it to be divisive. Nor did He give tongues to the Church to be ignored, shunned and classified as "unimportant."

Throughout the years, people have dug in on their doctrinal positions regarding tongues. Denominations, pastors and churches have strong convictions both for and against this subject. Due to the controversy that surfaces with tongues, many ministers and churches avoid discussing it openly. Oftentimes, they won't even discuss it in private. Therefore, people are left "in the dark" and have to draw their own conclusions.

We desperately need understanding on this essential gift. The explosive reactions to tongues virtually prove there is more to it than a simple take-it-or-leave-it topic of the Bible. The devil wants to continue to keep the body divided and clouded with confusion. Proverbs 4:7 says, *"Wisdom is the principle thing, but in all your getting get understanding."*

I remember as a Southern Baptist pastor how I publicly mocked those who spoke in tongues. I minimized its importance and discouraged all I could to avoid its practice. I openly questioned its current necessity in our biblical dispensation. I agreed it was necessary in the early developmental days of the New Testament church, but argued passionately that tongues had no relevance to the modern church and our contemporary lives.

However, after a close, meticulous study of the scriptures, I came to the conclusion that the baptism with the Holy Spirit and speaking in tongues were Biblical and still for us today. So, the very same Southern Baptist pastor that mocked the usage of tongues experienced it in all of its power and dynamic strength! To this day, it is an essential element to my walk with Christ.

I am so excited about this book. It will help you understand the purpose and extraordinary value of tongues, and therefore, prepare your heart, mind and spirit to receive and release the powerful ministry of tongues in your life.

Chapter Five

BORN SPEAKING IN TONGUES

One hundred twenty people are gathered in a tightly packed room anticipating the coming of the Holy Spirit. Ten days earlier, Jesus had instructed them to go to Jerusalem to wait on the promise of the Father, the Holy Spirit (Acts 2:42). On the fiftieth day after Jesus' supernatural resurrection it happened, the Holy Spirit dramatically descended on the disciples with explosive manifestations.

The first thing given to the first church on the first day was tongues. Mahesh Chavda, senior pastor of All Nations Church, Fort Mill, SC, said, "The

Church was born speaking in tongues."[10]

What a powerful word picture!

Of all the things God could have given the Church on opening day, He chose tongues. Isn't this amazing? This simple act should reveal to us the enormous value God places on speaking in tongues.

What is also remarkable, *everyone* in the first church spoke in tongues, all one hundred twenty of them (Acts 2:4).

God is both opportunistic and thorough. Understand, every act of God is intentional and carries purpose. He knew that praying and speaking in tongues would greatly benefit His precious followers. He also knew it was a way to magnify Christ and help the Church to share the gospel around the world.

Even from the beginning, speaking in tongues was controversial and disruptive. For example, the city people of Jerusalem who observed the disciples' outward display of tongues responded both negatively and positively. Some in the crowd that gathered to observe were confused by what they saw and heard. Others were amazed, and

---

[10] Mahesh Chavda, *The Hidden Power of Speaking in Tongues*, Destiny Image Publishers, Inc., 2003, pg. 11.

many marveled. The Bible adds, some in the gathering were perplexed, while others mocked and even accused them of being drunk (Acts 2:6-7, 12-13).

Things haven't changed much in two thousand years. Don't believe me? Let someone speak in tongues in a church where it is not taught.

Seriously, watch what happens, observe the reactions. Some would be amazed and marvel, while others would be deeply distraught, confused, perplexed, mad, and might make all kinds of accusations against the person speaking in tongues. The people in the church would demand answers and would want this activity to stop.

Someone has to ask the question, "If tongues was a key and necessary component to launch the Church, and a consistent element and practice throughout the churches that Paul and the apostles planted, then why is it today that the gift of tongues is under-emphasized, if not completely ignored by many pastors, churches, denominations and movements?"

This is an excellent question and it must be honestly addressed.

FOR THEN, BUT NOT NOW...

Even now, speaking in tongues is shrouded with confusion and skepticism. Some people describe the practice as unnecessary, unbiblical, and even demonic.

It is frightening to see how far the Church has drifted from the New Testament pattern and, more specifically, the teachings of Jesus and Paul.

Many in the Church are too quick to forget that every one of Jesus' followers and those in the early church spoke in tongues, all of them. They understood the multifaceted value of this blessed privilege. They acted on the teachings of Jesus and the Apostle Paul, who said we would and should speak in tongues.

Jesus -
"...cast out devils and speak in new tongues." Mark 16:17

Paul -
"I wish you all spoke in tongues..."1 Corinthians 14:5

"Do not forbid to speak in tongues..." 1 Corinthians 14:39

Sadly, many theologians and pastors strongly believe and teach that the gift of tongues was necessary for the early believers, but not vital to today's Church. This conclusion has inadvertently crippled and grossly limited the work of God, both in individuals and churches.

Some well-meaning pastors and teachers even use the Word of God to make their point that tongues are no longer available and/or necessary for people of God.

You ask how I know this? Don't forget I was a Southern Baptist pastor, and I used to Word of God to defend my position that tongues were not for today.

"TONGUES WILL CEASE"

The number-one passage I used to discount the usage and practice of tongues was 1 Corinthians 13:8-10. I now know I grossly misapplied and misinterpreted this passage.

"Love never fails. But whether there are prophecies, they will fail; whether there are tongues, they will cease; whether there is knowledge, it will vanish away. For we know in part and we prophesy in part. But when that which is perfect has come, then that which is in part will be done away."

I aggressively latched onto the words that said, *"...whether there are tongues, **they will cease;**"* (v. 8). As you will see, I then applied my own timetable to "when" tongues should cease. The Bible says in the same verse, *"tongues will cease when….**that which is perfect shall come.**"*

I erroneously assumed the phrase in verse 10, *"...that which is perfect is come"* meant the Bible, the Word of God.

Contextually the phrase, *"...that which is perfect is come"* doesn't say or even imply that it is referencing the Word of God. I unfortunately projected my theological preference, presuppositions, and, might I add, my prejudices upon the text.

We have used this text to tell our congregations that when the Word of God came to the body of Christ that *tongues*, *words of knowledge*, and *prophesy* would no longer be needed.

Our careless presumptions and reckless interpretation of this text have led millions, if not billions, of people over the years away from the blessed experience of speaking in tongues. In doing so, we have severely impeded the cause of Christ around the world.

I invite you to inspect 1 Corinthians 13 and see if there is the slightest reference or suggestion that, when the written Word of God comes into its fullness, the gifts of tongues, knowledge, and prophesy will no longer be necessary in the

Church. Look and see if you can pinpoint the place where it says it. Go ahead, search for it. You can't find it.

An honest hermeneutical and exegetical study of the passage reveals exactly what Paul was referencing when he said, *"when that which is perfect shall come...."*

He was pointing to the fact that it was **Jesus and His appearing.** The *"that which is perfect"* is Jesus. Paul WAS NOT referencing the scriptures, and more specifically, the canonization of the Bible. It clearly refers to, *"then **face to face**"* as being *"when that which is perfect shall come."*

The question is, "Was Paul talking about a document or a person?" The answer: A person. Not just any person, but Jesus.

Therefore, when we are united with Jesus *"face to face"* it will not be necessary for us to prophesy. When He is in our presence, there will be no need to have words of knowledge for others, nor any reason to speak in tongues. Why? He will be with us, *"face to face."*

Simply put, when we are in heaven we will not need the gifts of the Spirit to be in operation. All things will be perfect. We will know as we are known, the scripture says (1 Corinthians 13:12). The supernatural gifts of the Spirit are given to us now and are available for our ministry on the earth. This will be the case until we meet Him "face to face."

Over the years, religion has tried to minimize, if not eliminate tongues altogether. But note this one fact - God will always have a people who will believe the whole counsel of God; there will always be a remnant that will pray in tongues and operate in the gifts of the Spirit. They will refuse to bow their knee to the confining religious spirit that says tongues are not for today.

Chapter Six

VARIOUS TYPES OF TONGUES

A little boy opened the old and big family Bible with fascination. He was amazed as he looked at the pages and carefully turned them. Suddenly, to his surprise, something fell out of the Bible. He picked it up and looked at it closely. It was an old leaf from a tree that had been pressed between the pages.

"Momma, look what I found," the boy called out.
"What have you got there, Dear?" his mother asked.

With astonishment in the young boy's voice, he answered: "I think it's Adam's suit!'"

I heard it said recently, "You don't know what you don't know." The boy simply didn't know where the leaf came from, but now he does. Knowledge is power.

In this chapter, my goal is clear. I want to bring understanding and remove the confusion regarding tongues. I don't mean to come across as critical or condescending, but far too many in the body of Christ have a limited understanding of the subject of speaking in tongues. Therefore, there is a good possibility that what they do know is half correct or altogether incorrect. And because of this, they are not utilizing to the fullest this precious resource God has given to them.

The wisest man who ever graced the planet outside of Jesus was Solomon, and he penned these words three thousand years ago:

> *"Wisdom is the principal thing;*
> *Therefore get wisdom.*
> *And in all your getting,*
> *get understanding."*
> Proverbs 4:7

If any one topic of the Bible needs to be understood by Christians it is "tongues." I want to elevate your walk and encounter with the Holy Spirit. Therefore, I am going to dissect this subject and bring understanding to you.

Let's begin.

When Solomon said, *"in all your getting get understanding,"* he was challenging us to know thoroughly how things function and their purpose.

Practically, it literally means to be able to "grasp and comprehend." In short, understanding means, the ability to know how something works, how it is put together and why it exists.

For example, an electrician has "understanding" how electricity functions, its purpose and its dangers. A car mechanic knows all the nuances on what makes an engine work and what causes the car to break down. A teacher understands what is necessary in order to help a child read. I want you to have a solid Biblical understanding of tongues, to fully grasp how God wants tongues to be used in your life and in the Church.

For starters, what most people don't realize, is, there are more than just one type of tongues. And according to the Bible, tongues are used for more than one purpose.

Paul said in 1 Corinthians 12:10

"*to another the working of miracles, to another prophecy, to another discerning of spirits, to another different kinds of tongues, to another the interpretation of tongues.*"

If you don't understand that there are variations of tongues mentioned in the Bible, then you will have a difficult time accepting that God wants you to speak in tongues. You will limit its usage to a special someone God uses to speak out loud in a church service and therefore, feel it is not meant for you.

Let's look at the latter part of verse 10. "...*different kinds of tongues.*" The key word is "variations" and "different" kind of tongues.

The Bible breaks down tongues into two groups, private and public. Each group has two different usages of tongues.

GROUP ONE: PUBLIC TONGUE

This tongue is referenced as a spiritual gift in 1 Corinthians 12:10, and there are two ways the public tongue is used. The public tongue is typically used within a group of people, in public.

1. It is used as SIGN TO THE UNBELIEVER (1 Corinthians 14:22)

> *"Therefore, tongues are for a sign, not to those who believe but to unbelievers..."*

When God uses a person with this gift, they supernaturally speak another language that the individual has never been formally trained to speak. The unbeliever hears the person speak in their specific dialect. It is a message about God, His love, or perhaps a warning to the one hearing. The listener understands what is being said and usually becomes convinced God is real and He wants to save them.

You see this gift in operation in Acts 2:7-12.

*"Then they were all amazed and marveled, saying to one another, 'Look, are not all these who speak Galileans? And how is it **that we hear, each in our own language** in which we were born?… we do hear them speak in our tongues the wonderful works of God.' So they were all amazed and perplexed, saying to one another, 'Whatever could this mean?'"*

Here is the perfect example how this public tongue can work.

Pastor Mark Rutland traveled to Mexico to lead a crusade. When he arrived, he learned his translator fell ill and there was no one there that could interpret his message to the Mexican people.

Mark approached the platform and began to speak and, supernaturally, God enabled him to communicate in fluent Spanish with ease. As a result, the service went on, lives were changed, and, not surprisingly, people were saved.

2. It is used to get a SPECIFIC MESSAGE to the local church.

Throughout my years of ministry I have seen this gift in operation multiple times. It is very moving to realize that God, at times, has a direct message He wants to deliver to a specific congregation.

This is how it works: During a church service, a believer will yield to the Spirit's promptings and speak loudly in an *unknown* tongue so all can hear. Because it is an unknown tongue, no one understands what is being said; there is no clarity whatsoever. At the conclusion of the message in tongues, God will move upon someone else - or in some cases, upon the person giving the tongue - to render the interpretation. The message must be interpreted so the congregation can receive understanding and edification.

Interpretation of tongues is actually one of the gifts of the Spirit mentioned in 1 Corinthians 12:10.

Not everyone will be given this gift. You may go your whole life and never give or interpret a public tongue. This is perfectly fine. The Spirit gives this gift as He chooses (1 Corinthians

12:11).

GROUP TWO: PRIVATE TONGUE

1. The "private tongue" has more than one use. Let me explain.

The private tongue is to be used during your devotional or PERSONAL prayer time.

Paul identified this as a specific type of tongue and is completely different than the public tongue. Remember, the public tongue is used for a sign to the unbeliever and for church edification.

This tongue has been called by many "your private prayer language." In the text below, Paul specifically stated that tongues can be, and are to be, used to pray to God.

> "For if I **PRAY IN A TONGUE**, my spirit prays, but my understanding is unfruitful. What is the conclusion then? I WILL PRAY IN THE SPIRIT, and I will pray with the understanding. I will sing with the spirit and I will sing with understanding."
> 1 Corinthians 14:14-15

Personal prayer time can lead us into deep intercession, in which the Holy Spirit helps us pray effectively, even though we might not be fully aware of the things we are praying for. This is an amazing ministry of the Spirit of God in us.

Romans 8:26-27 reads,

> *"Likewise the Spirit also helps in our weaknesses. For we do not know what we should pray for as we ought, but **the Spirit Himself makes intercession for us** with groanings which cannot be uttered. Now He who searches the hearts knows what the mind of the Spirit is, because He makes intercession for the saints according to the will of God."*

Surely we all have experienced times of intercession, times when we felt an urgency to pray, or a need to stop everything we are doing and intercede on behalf of someone. Often it comes quickly and without warning. We find ourselves not knowing exactly what to pray or how to pray or what to say. We don't know how we "ought" to pray; i.e., we don't know the little, tiny, hidden details that are so very important.

All we know is, there is an irresistible pull to pray. That is when the Holy Spirit comes alongside us and *"makes intercession for us."* It means He partners with us while we are praying in tongues to literally push through the plan and will of God for a person or situation.

How does this happen?

The above passage in Romans tells us the Holy Spirit helps in our "weaknesses." The Greek word for *weaknesses* is *astheneia,* which may be translated as spiritually weak, and indicates one who does not know how to pray or what to pray, and even suggests being so feeble one does not want to pray! It is in times like these the Holy Spirit *helps* us.

The question is, exactly *how* does He *help* us?

The "help" the Holy Spirit offers is found in the original language used. This "help" involves coming *alongside* us in prayer, *grabbing hold* of the need at hand, and *pushing against* it with us. While we yield our spirit, the Holy Spirit makes intercession through us. He does not pray *instead* of the believer. He does not pray *for* the believer. He *assists* us in prayer.

The Holy Spirit "falls in with" the believer and takes hold of the situation at hand, helping the believer as he prays through the issue.

The Holy Spirit's role is much more than assisting us with praying in tongues. He also helps by reminding us of scripture so our prayers are backed with the Word of God. He helps by reminding us of promises that pertain to the situation. He often gives us a picture or a burden or desire that provides direction as to how to pray.

He also inspires us to keep praying, giving us strength to persevere. He will show us God's will so we can pray accordingly. The Holy Spirit will remind us that Jesus hears our prayers, giving us confidence that we are hitting the target. He will work in us faith, humility, and fervency as we pray. He supports, encourages, and leads the believer as he prays! These are the ways He *helps us as we pray.*

In his book, *The Reality of Prayer,* E.M. Bounds said, "The greatest and the divinest of all helpers is the Holy Spirit. He takes hold of things for us. We are dark and confused, ignorant and weak in many things, especially in the simple service of prayer. There is an 'ought' on us, an obligation, a necessity to pray, a spiritual necessity upon us of the most absolute and imperative kind. But we do not feel the obligation and have no ability to meet it. The Holy Spirit helps us in our weaknesses, gives wisdom to our ignorance...and changes our weakness into strength. The Spirit Himself does this. He helps and takes hold with us as we tug and toil. He pleads for us and in us. He quickens, illumines, and inspires our prayers. He elevates the matter of our prayers and inspires the words and feelings of our prayers. He works mightily in us so that we can pray mightily. He enables us to pray always and ever according to the will of God."

2. Your communion with God by the private use of tongues is also to be applied to WORSHIP of the Lord

It is a beautiful thing to be able to worship the Lord while singing in tongues. Paul said, "*...I will sing with the spirit and I will sing with understanding*" (1 Corinthians 14:15).

Again, Paul said he will sing "*with the spirit.*" This means Paul would be singing in tongues from his spirit. Not only does God encourage us to pray in tongues, He also wants us to worship in tongues! The depth of this truth has yet to be fully realized by believers. Not much is spoken in scripture about worshiping in tongues. However, Paul set a great example for us to follow.

I challenge you to yield your spirit and begin worshipping Jesus in tongues.

I understand if, at this point, you are somewhat confused or startled, but hang on; before long, it will all make perfect sense. The reason you may be a little befuddled is that the very idea of praying in tongues confounds our natural reasoning and basic understanding of "how" we are supposed to pray. It seems illogical, senseless and borderline flaky.

For clarification, the private prayer tongue is

completely different than the public tongue. Again, the emphasis is on prayer.

Paul says, *"I will pray in a tongue..."* (v. 14). He doesn't apologize, try to hide, or minimize its importance. No, it is exactly the opposite. He proclaims this is what he is going to do; "I am going to pray in a tongue."

The Bible brazenly declares that tongues should not be one dimensional. Paul introduces to us that tongues have a broader use. Do you see that now?

Later in this book you will not only see the benefits of praying in the Spirit, but also the importance.

Chapter Seven

A DISTURBING TREND

My ministry allows me to travel to various churches throughout the world, and recently I have observed a disturbing trend. There are more and more people within "Spirit-filled/Charismatic/Pentecostal" churches that do not speak in tongues.

It leads us to ask, how did this happen, and perhaps more importantly, why are so many non-spirit-filled people attending and participating in various levels of leadership in tongue-speaking churches.

One obvious reason is that people are seeking more than what they are getting from their traditional church experience. In addition, I believe they are attending and participating in these churches because they love the atmosphere, emotion, music, freedom, altar calls, enthusiasm, and the unpredictability of what is happening - and possibly, going to happen - during a church service.

Many of them, for the first time in their church life, find themselves in an environment that is being led, in real time, by the Spirit of God. This is typically opposite of the well oiled and finely tuned church service they are used to.

Even though they might not understand everything that is going on around them, they like the suspense and oftentimes, may I say, the spiritual dynamics taking place.

The good news is, they are involved in a Spirit-filled church, but the bad news is, for whatever reason many of them have yet to experience the baptism with the Holy Spirit and speaking with other tongues.

How do I know this trend is prevalent and increasing? When I give altar calls at other churches, I often ask people if they have been baptized with the Holy Spirit and whether they speak in tongues.

Increasingly, more and more people are answering, "No."

It's not all their fault!

You may be wondering how people can be in a "SPIRIT-FILLED" church and not be "filled with the Spirit."

There are several reasons for this trend.

Pastors are not teaching and preaching enough on the necessity of praying in tongues. Therefore, people draw the only logical conclusion - speaking in tongues must not be that important. Consequently, they develop a spiritual deficiency and lack of understanding regarding the seriousness and value of tongues.

Inadvertently, if a person has attended a spirit-filled church for a considerable amount of time, people assume that that individual prays in tongues. In some cases, I have noticed that many people are embarrassed to admit they haven't spoken, or currently don't speak, in tongues.

They keep it quiet because they don't want the "others" to know they are not "Spirit-filled." It is their secret.

They do everything else a Spirit-filled person does: raise their hands, shout, clap, and cry, etc. This scenario is real. They look and act the part, but don't speak in tongues.

In my travels I have also learned that many desire to speak in tongues and have sought it diligently to no avail. There seems to be a block. With all their soul and heart, they long to have this experience. However, it hasn't happened.

Some get frustrated and are tired of trying, and adopt the posture, "Well, I have asked and God knows my heart. If He wants me to have it, then He will give it to me."

So, they wait and wait, and nothing happens.

Not long ago, in Florida, I was at a church sharing how God was touching and changing lives in the baptismal waters at the North Georgia Revival in Dawsonville, Georgia. At the conclusion of my message, I invited people to come forward to be baptized. That night over 240 people responded to the invitation to meet Jesus in the water.

We started baptizing at 9:30 PM and continued to 9:30 the next morning. Over eighty people received their prayer language when they were baptized in the water.

The next day the pastor said to me, "Todd, I had no idea so many of my people have not been baptized with the Holy Spirit with the evidence of speaking in tongues."

IT IS A NEW DAY!

The day of not encountering His full power in your life, and simply wishing for it happen, is coming to a close. God is vigorously calling you out of the shadows. He knows where you are and is compelling you to come out of your hiding place.

At all costs, pursue this encounter with all your heart and allow nothing to distract and/or prevent you from what He has for you.

Chapter Eight

THE HOLY SPIRIT FALLS IN A PUBLIC HIGH SCHOOL

Soon after revival broke out in our church in Dawsonville, Georgia, I was asked by a pastor in Southeast Georgia to come and baptize people in his church. He also arranged a time that I would speak to an energetic group of public high school students that were studying Bible Literature.

I was told Sid Roth, who is the Founder and Director of the famous "It's Supernatural Network" and television show would join me in the classroom. This was going to be quite an honor to minister alongside Sid Roth.

My assignment was clear. I had twenty minutes

to share about all the spectacular miracles and encounters people were having with God in the water at the North Georgia Revival.

Sid's role was to share the gospel message to the students.

When Sid began his talk, it was evident God's hand was on him. He spoke with astonishing authority and clarity. The students were dialed in and listening to every word. He shared his testimony and then gave an opportunity for them to be saved. Several repented of their sins and became born again. What he did next - well, I was not expecting it!

As soon as he led them to Christ, he boldly proclaimed, "Now, God wants to baptize you with the Holy Spirit, with the evidence of speaking in tongues."

Can you believe that? Right there in the middle of a public high school classroom he was going to lead teenagers into the baptism with the Holy Spirit. I was startled, in fact, shocked. I was more than curious on how this was going to end up. To be honest, I didn't have much faith for this.

Without wavering, He instructed them all to lift their hands and, with heavenly boldness, he led them in a prayer to receive the fullness of the Holy Spirit.

When he said, "Amen," he gave the command of faith and said, "Be filled with the Holy Spirit."

Right there in a government institution, I saw the Holy Spirit come upon these students. It was an impressive sight to behold. I was amazed!

Then Sid went to the next level with it. Oh yes he did!

Immediately, with great faith, as if he knew what was about to happen, he told them to start speaking in tongues. Yes! He instructed them to release their prayer language and start speaking from their spirit. He even said, "Move your tongue and start saying something; blabber if you have to and God will take over."

I watched it all unfold right in front of me. These precious young people started speaking in tongues. God's presence was in the room. It was beautiful, supernatural, and so refreshing to see Sid do exactly what the Apostle Paul would have done.

I love his instruction, "...start speaking and blabber if you have to...." (I disagree with this)

If you want to pray in tongues, yield yourself to the Lord, don't speak in English. By faith, speak whatever comes up in your spirit; give sound to it.

Trust Him and let it flow.

Chapter Nine

FLIP THE SWITCH

(How to Maximize Praying in Tongues)

Turning on the light in your room is easy; flip the switch. The room goes from dark to light. And, whenever you leave the room, you flip the switch again and the light goes off.

Praying in the Spirit is activated in your life by "flipping the switch." I will explain below.

The Apostle Paul made it clear that he, author of two-thirds of the New Testament, prayed in tongues. He wasn't ashamed of it and understood the immense value of praying in the

Spirit.

1 Corinthians 14:5 *14:15*

> *"I will pray with the spirit, and I will also pray with the understanding. I will sing with the spirit, and I will also sing with the understanding."*

In this text, he noted two separate types of praying.

A. Praying with UNDERSTANDING

B. Praying in TONGUES

According to him, there is a considerable difference between the two.

When Paul prayed with "understanding" he prayed in his native language. He understood every word he was praying. How? He was praying with and from his brain.

His thoughts and words were developed first in his brain and then came forth out of his mouth. We all know every word we speak in our native language has its origin in our brain, and in a nanosecond, it gets transferred to our mouth and we give voice to the thought.

Praying in tongues is different. Paul explains

what takes place when he prays in tongues *"...my spirit prays."* Then he adds, *"my understanding is unfruitful."*

Why is that significant? Paul is intentionally differentiating and identifying two ways to pray - with understanding and without understanding (tongues).

When Paul says his spirit prays and that his understanding is unfruitful, he is letting us know that his mind and brain are not involved when praying in tongues. He identifies how this is possible: *"My spirit prays."*

Once more, we learned in school that the brain is the birthplace of all words. Therefore, when you pray in English or in your native language, it first starts in your brain.

But, when you pray in tongues, the words don't come from your brain, but from your spirit. Your spirit is now the birthplace of the words that will come out of your mouth. Next, your tongue gives sound to those words. It will make no sense to your natural mind. That's perfect! It isn't supposed to. It isn't meant to be logical.

Again, Paul said,

"For if I pray in a tongue, my spirit prays, but my understanding is unfruitful."

1 Corinthians. 14:14.

I want to make sure you understand that your spirit has a voice just like your brain. But, it can't be heard unless it comes out of your mouth.

Let's use the analogy introduced at the beginning of this chapter. I believe it will help you to begin praying in tongues.

Most of the time as you walk into a room, on a wall near the door is a light switch. You decide if you want the light on or off. Praying either in tongues or with understanding is like "flipping a switch." You decide which one and when.

Here is the beautiful thing: whenever I desire, I can pray with understanding or choose to pray in tongues.

You ask, "How is that possible?"

If I want to pray with understanding, I simply connect my tongue to my brain; this comes naturally. If I want to pray in tongues I have to "flip the switch." In doing so, I have to be purposeful and intentional. When I "flip the switch," I connect my tongue to my spirit. It's that simple, and the more you do it, the easier it is.

When you "flip the switch" and begin to pray in tongues, you are giving way to the Spirit of God to directly influence your prayers. In addition, it keeps your prayers from being tainted by the flesh, its lusts and wayward desires that are not the will of God for you.

If you and I will be honest, some, if not a large part of our praying in English (native language) is done outside of the will of God. Paul addressed this weakness we each have, in James 4:3, when he said, *"You ask and do not receive, because you ask amiss, that you may spend it on your pleasures."*

By dreadful experience, I know much of our praying in English is not congruent with the plan of God for our lives. We ask and petition God for things that are not in alignment with His perfect will.

Praying in tongues eliminates this frailty altogether.

Chapter Ten

GET FULLY DRESSED!

Can I make a confession? I don't like to shop, especially with my wife.

I know that sounds bad. I always love being with my wife, but it's the whole shopping thing that sends me over the edge. It is the "in and out" of every store that gets to me. Oh my goodness, if you want to severely torment me, make me walk the mall and follow my wife as we visit every rack of clothing, every clearance sale, shoe store and accessory counter.

Please, oh Lord, help me! At times I think even "goodness and mercy" refuses to follow me in the mall.

Like a lot of women, my wife loves to buy new

things, lots of new things. I often ask her why she needs to buy another pair of black pumps. I innocently add, "You have nine other pairs of shoes that look exactly like those in that box."

As she tilts her head twelve degrees and opens her mouth slightly, she stares straight at me as if she can't believe I would ask such a dumb question. If and when she does get around to responding, I never get a straight answer. I get the run-around of some sort and by the time she gets through explaining the various styles, textures, and other nuances to me I am so confused, worn out and mentally broken down that I end up sitting on a bench in the middle of the mall next to a total stranger, talking about milking cows or something like that.

By observing my wife, I have learned that women, to their credit, have a built-in ability to make men think they are winning an argument, but in the end we never do. We walk away feeling good, but within minutes we think to ourselves, "Wait, what just happened?" It may be the stall, pause, and stare-at-the-husband approach that works every time. It is like it's a part of their DNA. It is so natural.

As the hours drag on, she comes out of the store. I notice she has several bags. I also, know, the real reason I am with her is to tote the bags. As always, she gets a couple of new shirts, a few pairs of pants, glistening accessories, and new shoes. And to make me feel better she brings me a peace-offering. She comes out of the store smiling and approaches the bench and waits on me to finish my dialogue with Bert the Barber and says, "I bought you something."

At this point I am excited, thinking while I was visiting with my new friend she went to Bass Pro Shop or someplace like that. My hopes are high. Perhaps it's a tool, gun, ammo, anything usable, or a fun gadget of some sort. Nope. Not a chance.

She hands me the bag and it's a six-pack of t-shirts and underwear. Bob the Barber looks at me. We make eye contact. No words are exchanged. I take the bags off her arms and walk quietly behind her.

I love the quote by Carrie Bradshaw who said, "I like my money right where I can see it...hanging in my closet."

Another person said, "I could give up shopping, but I am not a quitter."

Speaking of clothing, the Word of God tells us we should suit up each day with the armor of God.

A closer look at tongues will reveal that praying in tongues is an intricate part of the armor of God.

What if I told you that, if you are not praying in the Spirit (tongues), you are not wearing all of the armor of God.

According to Ephesians 6:18, if we do not pray in tongues we are not taking advantage of the full complement of battle gear that God makes available to us. Have you ever thought about that?

It is true. It is like going to war without all of your armor and weaponry. In the natural we wouldn't dare do it. However, far too often, this is what happens to us as believers.

Let's be practical about this, shall we? The Bible uses the phrase "praying in the Spirit" to refer to praying in tongues (1 Corinthians 14:15; Jude 20; Ephesians 6:18). People ask, "Can you pray in your native tongue and be led by the Spirit?"

The answer is, "Yes you can." However, Paul connects praying in the Spirit with tongues (E.G., 1 Corinthians 14:14; Romans 8:26-27).

Far too frequently, Christians are losing battles in their personal lives and seem to be unprepared to face life's issues. This deficiency may be due to us not praying enough in the spirit (tongues). It is possible that the struggles and defeat in our lives could be because we do not have this piece of the armor on each day.

I don't know if you have noticed it or not, but too many of us seem to be living our Christian faith from the position of needing to attain another breakthrough rather than from the position of victory? Could it be we are fighting with inferior equipment or not all of our equipment?

Is it possible that we are abiding in a place of captivity and defeat rather than a position and posture of authority and strength?

Think about it: we get up every day to go into a dark world, a world where the devil seeks to devour us, a world where temptation lurks at every turn. The lust of the flesh, the pride of life, and lust of the eyes constantly put pressure on us to indulge our fantasies and lusts.

If we go into this hostile war zone without armoring up, then we are left to rely on our flawed intuition and our fleshly strength.

Even if we "make it through" the day without totally blowing it, there is still the other factor: there were great ministry opportunities that presented themselves to us.

For example, Rick the mail clerk: his daughter has leukemia; you wanted to help but didn't know what to say.

Then there was Jenny, who was grieving the passing of her mom. Again, your heart wanted to help, but you felt you would make things worse by mentioning it.

Then you saw Mark. This one tore you out of the frame. You have played golf together for years and you are close friends. He told you today that they found a mass on his liver and the early indication is that it is cancer. He was devastated, and tears came to his eyes as he shared the news with you. He held it together and there you sat, wanting to help, wanting to make it better, but you had nothing - just a few words of encouragement, but nothing else. You got in the car and you felt useless.

You did all you could do. You were kind and thoughtful, and that mattered. But can't we offer more? Isn't it possible to bring more to the battle than a polite, "I'm praying for you"?

Where is the power? Where is the Mark 16 manifestation in our lives? Why isn't it happening? Where is the "Silver and gold, I don't have, but WHAT I DO HAVE I GIVE TO YOU. RISE UP AND WALK!"?

This doesn't come because you are in church and/or go to a church that believes that it is available. I can't make it happen for you. I can't, as bad as I want to. I can't speak it over you and expect you to "get it." It comes when we prepare ourselves for war. It comes when we discipline ourselves to pray in the Holy Spirit for extended periods of time. We have to take this seriously. There is no shortcut, no quick tap on your head by a pastor or altar worker.

It only comes when we give ourselves to prayer and study of the Word (Acts 6:4).

Our approach to prayer has to change. We don't need to posture ourselves to survive, but to be successful for the Kingdom of God.

When we make the adjustment to consistently pray in tongues and give ourselves to His Word, we won't have to search for sermons and worship songs that encourage us to "hang on for another day." Nor will we constantly have to get in the prayer lines of anointed leaders just so we can "get our breakthrough."

Don't misunderstand me; all of the above are helpful and necessary. However, they cannot be a shortcut to your spiritual development and usability.

All believers would live so much more triumphantly if we understood what is available to us, and utilize it.

The gift of tongues is a piece of the warrior's armament. It should not be ignored. The battle is coming to you. Broken lives walk by you each and every day, people who are shattered and on the verge of devastation. How will you respond? Will it be about your survival, your needs, your breakthrough? Or, will you be ready to go to war for someone else?

As a pastor, I have observed that very rarely do believers who pray every day in tongues come in for counseling. Do they need encouragement from time to time? Of course, we all do.

But for them, each week isn't about climbing out of an avalanche of defeat and hopelessness. They have learned how to BUILD themselves up and have put on spiritual muscle so that when the battle comes, they are already trained and prepared for the conflict.

Chapter Eleven

ADDRESSING YOUR MISUNDERSTANDINGS

"Dear God, thank you for the baby brother, but what I prayed for was a puppy."

I think that is so funny. Evidently the child thought God misunderstood her request.

Through experience, we all know how easy it is to misunderstand someone's words, and we also know what it is like to be misunderstood.

What does it mean to misunderstand something? Simply put, it is a failure to comprehend the issue at hand correctly.

If there is one subject that Christians don't fully

understand, it is "tongues." If you don't believe me, start up a conversation about tongues with your friends. Listen to what they say; it will blow your mind.

If a person does not work through their misunderstandings of speaking in tongues, chances are, the confusion will remain and they will not experience the riches of speaking in tongues.

I get it. No one intentionally wants to misunderstand things. It is usually due to not having accurate information, or perhaps mishearing something that is being said. A misunderstanding can seem to be valid, and even logical. My goal in this chapter is to remove the fog in order to prepare the way for you to speak in tongues.

Below are a few misunderstandings we have regarding speaking in tongues.

A. I Don't Want it to Be Me "Making it Up!"

Believe me, I appreciate this so much. I completely understand you want this blessed experience to be "all God" and fully and completely His doing. I am thankful you don't want anything conjured up. So, you have thought or even said the following:

I don't want it to be me.
I don't want it to be made up.
I don't want it to be my flesh.

Even though your heart is in the right place, this thinking has the potential to develop into spiritual paralysis. It may seem noble and wrapped-up in "spiritual reasoning and pretense," but actually it is counterproductive to your walk with God and your effectiveness as a believer.

I know it sounds like I am speaking from both sides of my mouth, but it is true that we have to act on faith. And Paul declared that receiving the promise of the Spirit is by faith. (Galatians 3:14)

Think about it. Every time you pray in English, it has the strong potential to be the very thing you don't want praying in tongues to be: **"Made up."**

Let me explain. When you pray in English, it is you. You make it up, think it up, your prayers are first generated in your mind - it comes from you. You see that, right?

In prayer, when you ask for a new job, you made that up. I'm not saying it is wrong, I'm just saying it came from your mind, a point of need, it was your thought and you verbalized it to the Lord.

Again, it is commendable to use the logic, "I want it to be all God." However, sadly, I believe many use this as an acceptable escape for not aggressively pursuing tongues, and thus acquit themselves of any responsibility.

Over the years I have seen it hundreds of times. A person will come to the front sincerely desiring to pray in tongues. In their heart they are so pure and they do not want it (praying in tongues) to have anything to do with them, they want it to be "all God."

With uplifted hands and tears in their eyes they will say, "I want to speak in tongues." Then they will slightly open their mouth waiting for words and the supernatural prayer language to suddenly come forth, to leap out of their mouth. They want the Spirit to take their tongue and start formulating words for them.

This is not how praying is done, either in your native language or your spirit language. Acts 2:4 says, "...*as they spoke, the Spirit gave them the utterance.*" It involves us; we must flip the switch and connect our tongue to our spirit and begin to give voice to the utterances coming forth.

Many are concerned they won't do it right, or they will mess it up. Let me encourage you - you can't and won't mess it up. Here is why.

Whenever a child begins to speak, it struggles to formulate words. In the beginning they are literally pushing out words the best they can. At first they just make sounds. For example, a little boy sees a toy car on the table; he can't quite reach it so he will point to it and say, "Uh, uh."

The mom, without hesitating, will reach for the car and as she gives him the car she says to him, "car." The parent doesn't shame him, mock him, or discourage him. Why? He is pushing out his new language and the parent knows this and celebrates every syllable.

A neighbor who is not familiar with your child will hear the same thing and go, "What does he want? I don't understand what he is saying." But you, his parent, know his language!!!!

People also believe they should speak fluently in this new language right from the start. And, if they don't they may feel it wasn't real or that something is wrong with them. All language has a starting point and it grows over time. Just like with any language, the more you use it the more it grows and develops.

Push it out!

B. Tongues is Only for a Few People

In other words, people believe speaking in tongues is not meant for everyone.

Paul asked a question, *"Do all speak in tongues?"* He responded, "No."

Before you jump to the conclusion that your point is validated by Paul that not everyone is meant to speak in tongues, we need to clarify what type of tongues the Apostle Paul was referring to.

Again, based upon his question and the answer he implied, far too many people come to the erroneous conclusion that tongues are not for everyone. But one needs to take a closer look at the context of the question.

Remember, earlier we correctly learned there are variations of tongues, public and private. The public tongue is to be used as a sign for the unbeliever and for the edification of the local church body; this type of tongue is not meant for everyone. However, the private prayer tongue is for all (1 Corinthians 12:28-30).

Once again, Paul is addressing the spiritual gift of tongues that God has set in the church for public ministry. In order to make his point that not all have the gift of "public" tongues he also establishes not everyone is an apostle, prophet, teacher, worker of miracles. (1 Corinthians 12:29-30). In this list, he mentions speaking in tongues or interpretation of heavenly languages.

For clarity, when Paul said, "Do all speak in

tongues?" he was referencing the public tongue and not the heavenly prayer language which is available to everyone.

C. If God Wants Me to Speak in Tongues He Will Have to Make it Happen

Whenever a gift of the Spirit is in operation, you will discover that there is a partnership or cooperation between God and man. Each gift involves man's participation. For example, when we are led to witness to someone, the Spirit doesn't immediately take your tongue and start speaking words without your consent and cooperation. The Spirit of God works with you and through you.

The same is true with speaking in tongues.

J.E. Stiles, a Pentecostal evangelist and teacher of the 1940s and 50s, helped many people remove blocks to receiving the gift of tongues.

He wrote: "Very often it has been said, concerning speaking with tongues, 'The Holy Spirit speaks through the man.' Or to someone upon whom the Spirit was moving we have said, 'Now just let the Spirit speak through you.' These expressions convey the idea that the Holy Spirit actually does the speaking Himself. The fact is that this is not true. The Holy Spirit does not speak. The Word plainly teaches that the man

DOES the speaking, but the Spirit supernaturally DIRECTS it. (Acts 2:4) "[11]

"For if I pray in a tongue, my spirit prays..."
1 Corinthians 14:15

He adds, "The miracle is not in the fact that the man speaks, but in what he speaks. As long as a man speaks with other tongues, he has absolutely no control as to what he says. What he says is entirely supernatural."[12]

D. I am Afraid I Won't Be Able to Stop or Control It.

People falsely believe they will not be able to control praying in tongues. Many think the Spirit will override their mental faculties and possess them as if under some type of spell. Here is the truth: You can control it. You can start and stop praying in tongues anytime you like. Just as I can stop and start praying in English anytime I choose. It is about yielding your spirit, brain and tongue. Again, I can flip the switch on or off, anytime.

"And the spirits of the prophets are subject to the prophets." 1 Corinthians 14:32

---

[11] Dr. Brad Long, https://www.prmi.org/removing-obstacles-to-receiving-the-gift-of-tongues/
[12] Ibid.

Chapter Twelve

TEN BENEFITS TO PRAYING TONGUES

From time to time we get asked, "Why should I pray in tongues?" They simply want to know what will be the results and benefits.

Below are 10 fabulous benefits to praying in the Spirit.

1. You Pray the Perfect Will of God

This benefit may be the most important. Each time we pray in tongues we are allowing the Holy Spirit to lead us in our praying. How does that work? The Spirit is communicating directly with our spirit, and we give voice to His prompting through tongues. It is a beautiful arrangement: God working with man to pray His perfect will.

Another great question we get asked on occasion is, "If I am praying the perfect will of God, then why is there so much chaos happening in my life? Why do bad things still take place?"

We cannot forget we are in a war. Just as God is at work in your life, the enemy has raised an assault against you, as well. He has schemes and an aggressive agenda for you and your family. Imagine the devastation in our lives if we *didn't* pray the perfect will of God. Tongues are of utmost importance, especially in this day and age.

HERE IS A GREAT SUGGESTION

Think about all God could do in and through us if we prayed, uninterrupted, in tongues for thirty minutes a day? Oh, the level of glory and power that we would experience! The Church would advance the Kingdom with might and strength. Our lives would take on such clarity and we would walk in an unprecedented realm of peace. Start this today!

2. It is a Special Code of Communication

In every military engagement, essential high-level information must be shared with key personnel. A war can be quickly lost if troop movements, air strikes, rendezvous points, vital battle plans, etc., are not shared with the necessary leaders. In order to not have the delicate information detected and understood by the enemy a special language or code is put into place. This unique language or code is known by their side only, therefore, preventing the enemy from intercepting or subverting their plans.

A well known example of coded wartime communication is seen in the code talkers of World War II. The U. S. Army enlisted the aid of hundreds of Native Americans to develop coded messages in Navaho, Comanche and other tribal languages that were virtually unknown to the Axis powers, and succeeded in baffling enemy code breakers. Code talkers were a significant factor in the Allied forces winning World War II.

Praying in tongues is the Christian's special language. The enemy cannot break the code. I love how the Amplified Bible says it in 1 Corinthians 14:2:

"For one who speaks in an unknown tongue does not speak to people but to God; for no one understands him or catches his meaning, but by the Spirit he speaks mysteries [secret truths, hidden things]."

When we pray in tongues, the devil cannot understand or decipher what we are praying. It puts the devil at a disadvantage and in a reactive mode, responding to our advances. Again, this is a weapon the Lord has given us; let us take full advantage.

3. It Draws You Closer to God

You can actually use your spirit language for more than just praying. You can sing, worship and magnify God in tongues (Acts 2:11; 1 Corinthians 14:15).

There is a special intimacy that occurs when we pray in the Spirit, and there is no doubt that the more you pray in tongues the closer walk with the Spirit you will have. It is a by-product of yielding your spirit to the Spirit of God while in prayer.

Dave Roberson, author of, *"The Walk of the Spirit, The Walk of Power,"* said, "You're going to provoke an internal war when you begin to consistently pray in tongues, because impurities will soon start to surface that you don't want to get rid of. God will endeavor to purge those impurities off your life so you can fulfill your divine call without being destroyed by the devil."[13]

4. You Develop Your Spiritual Muscles

The more time we take with this special

---

[13] Dave Roberson, The Walk of the Spirit - The Walk of Power: The Vital Role of Praying in Tongues

opportunity, the less vulnerable we are to the temptations and wiles of the devil. We become stronger in the spirit as we exercise our spirit man. Paul told Jude in verse 20, *"But you, beloved, building yourselves up on your most holy faith, praying in the Holy Spirit..."*

When praying in tongues, your spirit is being built up and gains strength. That means you are literally putting on spiritual muscles. This is why some of the physically smallest and weakest among us appear as giants in the spirit to the devil. Those older lady saints that are no more than 100 pounds in the flesh are like valiant mighty warriors in the spirit. The devil doesn't want anything to do with them. He and his cronies scurry away when these precious saints begin to pray.

Again, praying in the Spirit is like working out your spiritual muscles. The more you do it, the stronger you become.

5. It Stirs Up Your Faith

Praying in tongues doesn't necessarily give you more faith, but it most definitely stirs it up.

After periods of prolonged praying in tongues, my faith is activated and supercharged. I feel extremely close to the Lord and believe that anything is possible. The same will happen to you if you will let it.

Kenneth Hagin once said, "Praying in tongues charges your spirit like a battery charger charges a battery."

6. You Supernaturally Accomplish More

How do I know this? The more time I pray in tongues, the more I am able to accomplish in life and for the Kingdom of God. Plus, I experience ease in my work.

Praying in tongues prepares you for your future and your future for you. In the process, obstacles and opposition are being uprooted and weakened even before you face them in the natural.

Remember, praying in tongues takes you beyond human capabilities and far beyond your earthly knowledge of things. Everything about praying in tongues is supernatural.

If I don't spend adequate time praying in the Spirit, I will have to work harder to accomplish God's purpose for my life. I will have to rely on my earthly analytical knowledge and strength - which oftentimes falls short of His best. Praying in tongues enlarges your capacity to do much more for the Lord than you ordinarily could.

7. It Gives You Rest and Peace

I can't tell you how many times I have been physically and spiritually exhausted, but after praying in the Spirit for about ten minutes, my body and spirit became rejuvenated. It is remarkable at how exuberant I have felt afterwards, as though I had taken a power nap.

Dave Roberson in his book, *The Walk of the Spirit,* said, "Praying in tongues is a priceless gift that God has given us so we can feel rested and refreshed right in the middle of a very imperfect world!"

"For with stammering lips and another tongue He will speak to this people, to whom He said, 'This is the rest with which You may cause the weary to rest.' And, 'This is the refreshing;' yet they would not hear." (Isaiah 28:11-12)

8. It Can Calm You in a Turbulent Environment

When chaos is rampant and the noise and distractions are unbearable, it is a perfect opportunity to pray quietly in tongues.

How does it work? As you pray in tongues, you subvert your flesh and place it under the control of the Spirit of God. Don't give in to the urge to become reactive and destructive. Commit your tongue to the Spirit and pray in tongues, and watch the stress level in your physical body diminish. The burden will be lifted. The release of peace and calm may take a few minutes as your flesh and ears respond to the activity in the room. Nevertheless, keep praying under your breath in the Spirit and watch with awe how His grace will work in your life.

9. It Opens the Gateway for Real-Time Ministry Opportunities.

Throughout your day, pray in tongues. Paul said, *"Pray without ceasing"* (1 Thessalonians 5:16). This doesn't mean you must pray nonstop twenty-four hours a day. That would be impossible. It means you should stay in a constant state of prayer, maintaining an awareness and posture of prayer. This is easier to do when you are baptized with the Holy Spirit and have a heavenly prayer language. In a nanosecond, you can be praying the perfect will of God for someone or something, and you are ready no matter what you encounter.

Often, when I am praying in the midst of my day, a thought or divine appointment will take place, and because I have been praying, the Lord will give me clarity on what I should say or do. It is such a blessing to *"walk in the Spirit"* (Galatians 5:16).

10. It Brings Clarity to the Will of God for Your Life

Praying in the Spirit removes the clutter that builds up in our minds, the kind of clutter that often prevents us from making wise and godly decisions. Praying in the Spirit minimizes confusion so that God's will becomes more apparent.

Once again, when I spend significant time praying in tongues, my mind is clearer, my discernment is sharper, and my decision making is more on point. Notice I said "significant time" praying in tongues. You simply cannot spend a minute or two a day in prayer and expect all of the above to happen. Commit yourself to establishing your prayer life and you will see your *entire* life improve.

In addition, you will become more productive for the Kingdom of God, as a higher level God-awareness will arise in your life.

I also have discovered some additional benefits to praying in the Spirit.

My joy is fuller.
My peace is more prevailing.
My sensitivity to the Spirit's promptings is heightened.
My love for people is deeper.

As you can see, the benefits of praying in the Spirit are multifaceted and rewarding.

Chapter Thirteen

WARNING: THE DEVIL WILL BE MAD

The famed evangelist and pastor, R.A. Torrey, said, "When the devil sees a man or woman who really believes in prayer, who knows how to pray, and who really does pray, and, above all, when he sees a whole church on its face before God in prayer, he trembles as much as he ever did, for he knows that his day in that church or community is at an end."

As stated above, Satan knows the power of prayer and will do everything within his power to discourage and prevent you from consistently praying.

Of all the people on the earth Satan hates, he hates the praying person the most. You are engaged in battle that weakens his strongholds and that advances the Kingdom of God.

Mother Teresa said, "God shapes the world by prayer. The more praying there is in the world, the better the world will be, the mightier the forces against evil."

Without reservation, I can say that Satan trembles when a child of God stands in front of the throne of God and, with faith, vigorously petitions the Lord to release His will upon the earth. Nothing on earth moves God to action like the cry of a son or daughter praying in faith. God loves it when His children pray!

However, you must know that the devil will fight you at every turn to keep you from praying in tongues. He will whisper to you that you are not making a difference and that praying in tongues is being "made up" by you. He will cause you to think it is all "gibberish" and nonsense. These are all lies from the enemy.

Also, you may at some point feel that praying in tongues is an unproductive use of your time. Because you don't know what you are saying, you might doubt that your prayers are being answered.

These types of attacks and thoughts are to be expected. Resist them and keep praying in the

Spirit. Don't stop! Press in all the more! The devil loathes a persistent spirit, someone that will not quit. If you stay with it, Satan will eventually leave you alone.

I love what Andrew Murray said regarding prayer: "O, let the place of secret prayer become to me the most beloved spot on earth."

And I love this scripture:

"Now My eyes will be open and My ears attentive to prayer made in this place."
2 Chronicles 7:15

Below are a few truths I want you to remember when you pray in tongues:

- You are praying God's perfect will to be done.

- You are sowing to the Spirit; therefore you will reap by the Spirit.

- You could be praying for someone on the other side of the world who needs you to pray. Their life could be in danger.

- You are interceding for and activating God's will on the earth.

- Every time you pray in tongues, the Kingdom advances.

- You are strengthening your own walk with God.

Chapter Fourteen

TWO REASONS THE DEVIL DOESN'T WANT YOU TO PRAY IN TONGUES

The Pew Research Center found that eighteen percent of Americans spoke in tongues at least several times a year.[14] Wow! Only two out of ten people pray in tongues. This statistic reveals a lot to us about the subject of tongues, such as:

1. It is still not accepted in the mainstream Church.

---

[14] The New York Times Sunday Review, April 17, 2013, "Why We Talk in Tongues" https://www.nytimes.com/2013/08/18/opinion/sunday/luhr mann-why-we-talk-in-tongues.html

2. The devil is working overtime to keep this blessed privilege away from as many believers as possible.

As we have previously discussed, tongues is the most divisive and confusing doctrine in the Church. The devil recognizes this and his plan is to keep it that way.

Below are other reasons I believe the devil wants to keep the Church in the dark regarding this beautiful gift.

PRAYING IN TONGUES OPENS UP HEAVEN OVER OUR LIVES AND MINISTRIES

Praying in tongues launches us into a realm of the Spirit that we have been destined to live in, the supernatural. Tongues is the golden key God has graciously given to His children and, if utilized, it will unlock the heavens over us.

Don't misunderstand me; a person can certainly be used by God if they don't pray in tongues. However, their lives and ministries can be even more powerful if they consistently pray in the Spirit.

Thomas Watson said, "Prayer delights God's ear; it melts His heart; and opens His hand. God cannot deny a praying soul."

Praying in tongues is your secret weapon! Utilize it.

Without doubt, a secret weapon will give you a tactical advantage over your enemy. Why? The enemy is unaware of what is going to happen.

Why is this important?

For starters, secret weapons are used to intimidate opponents. Secondly, they are used to either further one's cause or to prevent the enemy from advancing his purposes.

Praying in the Spirit accomplishes all three: providing a tactical advantage over the enemy by keeping him in the dark, intimidating the enemy and short-circuiting his cause. This is why the devil wants as few people as possible praying in tongues.

Sadly, life validates that the Holy Spirit and His activities are limited in our life when we don't consistently pray in the Spirit. The key word is "consistently." Each of us should pray in tongues daily, and often, throughout the day. This blessed privilege of praying in the Spirit is too precious not to do it regularly.

Here is why we should pray in tongues as often as we can:

IT OBLITERATES OBSTACLES TO GOD'S WILL

A dreadful thing sometimes happens on the battlefield. Soldiers who are patrolling a certain area may be completely unaware of landmines hidden around them. Those deadly mines are there to render huge swathes of territory impassable, thus, prohibiting the advancement of an approaching army.

For those who don't know what a landmine is, it is an explosive device that is designed to detonate when triggered by pressure or a tripwire. A landmine's purpose is to destroy or disable personnel and/or vehicles.

Demining or mine clearance is the process of removing landmines from a particular area. The ultimate goal is to find the hidden mines on the battlefield and successfully remove them so the troops can advance.

This is painstaking work and attention to detail is a must. Militaries have landmine removing capabilities, such as mine plows, metal detectors, robots, and blast waves.

The devil seeks to plant landmines strategically around us, our families, and our churches. His destructive plans and deadly devices are hidden, and if not correctly identified and appropriately removed, they can cause Christ's plans for our lives to be delayed, if not derailed altogether.

Praying in tongues releases the plans and purpose of God and, at the same time, goes a long way to uproot the devil's plans and schemes. The devil - just like God - has an agenda for every church service. A lot of bad can be prevented and a lot of great and miraculous things can be released if we will just take the time to pray in the Spirit.

On Saturday nights, it was the custom at our church to pray at 10 PM. A handful of spiritually hungry people would gather to seek God and to pray for His will to be done in the next morning's church service.

I could usually tell what kind of service we were going to have by the way we prayed. When deep travail and intercession would come upon us, I knew church was going to be explosive. I also noticed, when we prayed fervently in the Spirit with strong conviction and faith, it was as if the Spirit would go before us and clear the way, remove the devil's obstacles so God's will could be accomplished.

Truthfully, I discovered that powerful Sunday worship gatherings ultimately depended on our effort, focus and faith. If we half-heartedly prayed, the service was "okay," but not "dynamic," If we pressed in during prayer, we could always count on a mighty move of God's Spirit. Over a period of time we realized the Lord's purposes are won in prayer, and, for us, it was usually prayer that took place the night before.

"...*The heartfelt and persistent prayer of a righteous man (believer) can accomplish much [when put into action and made effective by God—it is dynamic and can have tremendous power]*." James 5:16

The main indicator of how powerful and successful our church meetings will be is directly proportionate to how much our congregation prays in tongues. The more we pray, the more we seek His face, the more dramatic God's manifestation is in our church and lives.

Let me encourage you to commit yourself to praying in tongues for your church, pastor, and family. It will clear the way for God to mightily move on their behalf.

Chapter Fifteen

CAN YOU PRAY FOR A FRIEND OR LOVED ONE WHILE PRAYING IN TONGUES?

The wonderful answer is, YES, you can!!!

This is how it works.

You can direct your spirit to pray in tongues for a particular person or situation at any time. Let me give you an example.

I can pray for my wife, Karen, in English and be perfectly effective. However, naturally speaking, it is impossible for me to know everything she is currently encountering. I may not be aware that she is in danger, requires wisdom regarding a decision she must make, or simply needs the Lord to minister to her. Because I don't know what I should pray for, the impact that praying with my understanding could be having on her life and situation is somewhat limited.

Let me reiterate a valuable point. If Karen is not physically with me, it is virtually impossible for me to know what she will encounter over the next five minutes. Understandably, my scope of awareness and familiarity with all that is taking place in her world is finite. Therefore, if I pray in English for her, I pray only what I know; subsequently, my influence on her situation is narrow.

The great news is that the Spirit of God knows all things, everything about her life and all that she currently needs. Even though I don't know what to pray for in the natural, I can pray for her in tongues. And when I do, I have the full assurance that I am praying God's perfect will for her life.

Paul said it this way,

> "*Likewise the Spirit also helps in our weaknesses. **For we do not know what we should pray for as we ought,** but the Spirit Himself makes intercession for us with groaning which cannot be uttered. Now He who searches the hearts knows what the mind of the Spirit is,*

because He makes intercession for the saints according to the will of God." Romans 8:26-27

Did you see that?

"For we don't know what we should pray for as we ought."

God knows we are painfully hampered due to our limited knowledge of the events that affect us and our loved ones. However, He didn't leave us without a solution. He gave us the Holy Spirit to help us. When we pray in tongues, the Spirit of God supernaturally directs our praying. He tells our spirit what to pray and then we pray it out in tongues, His perfect will.

On an extremely practical level, this is how you direct your tongues to benefit a particular person or situation:

Think of a person you love, or an issue that you or a friend is facing.

Lock that person or situation into your mind.

In English (native language) pray for them.

"Flip the Switch" and begin to pray from your spirit in tongues.

I do this all the time. I pray for the things I know, but then I "flip the switch" and begin to pray in tongues. I trust the Spirit to lead me to pray for things I don't know about or understand.

Whatever you do, please don't undervalue the blessed ability to pray in tongues for your family and friends. This could literally save someone's life. Your prayers could prevent a tragic accident and/or release angelic protection over a missionary in a foreign land. The impact you have when you pray in tongues is substantial. Paul knew this, so he encouraged the people of God to *"Pray without ceasing"* (1 Thessalonians 5:17).

Don't forget, it was the Apostle Paul who taught us to pray this way; he set the example. He encouraged people to utilize both praying in tongues and praying with understanding. He said,

"I will pray with understanding and in tongues."
1 Corinthians 14:15.

You can do this as often as you would like. It is possible, and it's simple. Try it now!

Chapter Sixteen

PRAY IN THE SPIRIT FOR THESE FOUR THINGS EVERY DAY

Consistency in prayer is essential. You are literally plowing up fallow ground when you pray. You are clearing the way for God's purposes to be accomplished.

Below are four areas God needs us to target in our praying.

1. Your WORK PLACE is your Mission Field

Your work is not just a "job" that provides for the needs of your family; it is much more. Your job gives you an opportunity for the light that is in you to penetrate the darkness. The Lord has strategically positioned you so you can take the great news of the Savior to those who may never go to church.

Even though you may not like your current job, and may only be there for a season, commit it to Him. The Bible says, *"The steps of the righteous are ordered by the Lord"* (Psalm 37:23).

If you believe this passage, then God has led you to where you are. I encourage you to view your job as your specific mission field. God, in His loving care for unsaved and hurting people, has coordinated the events of your life and directed your path so you could be in the lives of those precious souls around you.

Understand, God has sent you to a particular office or plant for His purposes. Make the most of it.

Here is how to make a huge impact at your place of work.

A. Your mindset has to be: "This is my mission field and my assignment is to bring love and light to this environment."

B. Ask God to fill your heart with compassion for all your work associates.

C. Pray for the people around you.

Here is the best way to do that: call out each of your colleagues by name before God, and then aggressively, with great faith, pray in tongues for them.

Every day, spend a few minutes praying for each one. Many of the people you work beside are walking through difficulties that you are not aware of: sickness, wayward children, dysfunctional home, a bad marriage, financial hardship, etc. You are important and God needs you to pray for them.

Think about this: out of the 7.6 billion people on the earth you may be the only person on the planet praying for them. War for them in prayer! Please realize that your prayers could literally be holding back the hordes of hell that are attacking them. Your intercession possibly could prevent their total destruction. Even greater, your prayers can and will clear the way for the gospel to find its way to them.

Don't give up on them, persevere.

2. Business Decisions and Purchases

Thousands, if not millions, of dollars could be saved if people would pray in tongues before making a business decision.

Every significant purchase or investment must be covered with prayer - not just prayer, but praying in tongues.

Remember, you are limited in your knowledge. You can't see the future; you don't know all things. But the Spirit of God does. He can warn you of problems ahead or grant you permission to proceed.

Jesus said, *"...the Spirit will guide you into all truth"* (John 16:13). This "truth" He speaks of isn't limited to truth about Jesus; it is much, much broader than that.

Things that could possibly mislead you or set you back can be averted by the Spirit of God, who can and will lead you into the truth. Jesus wants you and me to do the right thing. However, while doing the right thing is usually simple, it might not be easy. We sometimes get impatient and want to make quick decisions.

In order to be led into "truth," you and I have to be willing to commit the time in order to know the perfect will of God for our life and business.

For example, you can't pull into a car lot and test drive a car and then pray in tongues to see if it is okay by the Spirit to purchase the car. That is not how it operates. The praying needs to be done beforehand, so that before you pull onto the car lot you already know the will of God.

It is very easy to "feel" as though it is the will of God to purchase a car when you are sitting on the fine leather seats and enjoying all the new gadgets the new model car has to offer.

I know of many people who have gotten themselves into a situation because they felt it was God's will for them to purchase an automobile, but five months down the road, they admitted they made a mistake. They got "caught up" in a moment. They allowed their flesh to make the decision, rather than being led by the Spirit of God.

I believe many personal economic disasters could have been prevented if adequate time had been spent seeking God and praying in tongues.

Again, it is worth repeating: when you pray in tongues regarding a purchase, you must give God time to speak to you. Separate yourself from the noise, the emotion of the moment, then submit your will to His and honestly say, "I will do whatever You ask of me."

Tell the Lord – and mean it - that you would be ok if He told you "No." To walk in truth and His perfect will for your life, you must have no pretense. Your will and fleshly desires and wants must be laid down on the altar. It is then, and then only, that He will speak and direct and guide you into all truth.

3. Family and Significant Others

It is a *must* that we pray in tongues for our family members. Again, we don't know what each one will face throughout the day, but God does. We do know the devil walks about like a roaring lion seeking to devour.

Peter gave us this warning:

"Be sober, be vigilant; because your adversary the devil walks about like a roaring lion, seeking whom he may devour." 1 Peter 5:8

Praying fervently in the spirit releases the plan and protection of God into our loved ones' lives. It often prevents evil and defuses the full effect of catastrophic attacks.

For example, someone you know may have been in a horrific car accident and should have died, but your prayers may have saved their life.

We must take this seriously. The enemy will show no mercy on our family. Destruction is his ultimate goal. He will wreak havoc whenever he has an open door. We are not fearful of his strategy for our lives, but we are aware.

God has given us authority and provision to upset the devil's plans. However, if we are oblivious to his activities, his agenda may go unchecked and unhindered.

Jesus taught His disciples to pray a certain way: "*Your kingdom come, your will be done on earth as it is in heaven....*"

As a father and husband, it is my duty to pray over my family. I am like a watchman on the wall, ever observant to the maneuvers of the enemy. However, I am not only defensive in my posture in prayer. I am also proactive and assertive. I know God's will for my children and spouse. Therefore, I pray that all boundaries and obstacles be removed from their paths so the purposes of God can be accomplished in their life.

For example, my pre-emptive prayers for them include the removal and elimination of all wrong relationships, wrong influences, wrong decisions, etc. I also ask the Father to bring the right people and opportunities to them.

Furthermore, I pray in tongues over them for divine protection. I often pray like Jesus prayed for His disciples,

*"I do not pray that You should take them out of the world, but that **You should keep them from***

the evil one." John 17:15

Do you see how Jesus prayed? Jesus knew the enemy was coming for them, but prayed that they would be kept from him and his ways. We should follow the Lord's example.

Jesus even told Peter,

"*Simon, Simon! Indeed, Satan has asked for you, that he may sift you as wheat. **But I have PRAYED FOR YOU** that your faith should not fail....*" Luke 22:31-32

On a practical side, here is how to cover your child in prayer while praying in tongues.

If possible, have a picture of your child in front of you, or just have them on your mind. Ask the Lord to direct you as you commit five minutes to pray in tongues for your child. Yield completely to the Spirit of God and begin to pray in tongues. There will be times your prayer language will change. It may get more forceful, loud or even aggressive. This means you are combating, or preventing, and/or forcing something to happen in the Spirit.

When this takes place do not leave prematurely. Stay until peace comes. Don't pull away too soon. You are interceding and God needs you to stay with it until the job is complete in the spirit realm.

Don't panic or become fearful that something bad is about to happen; instead, rejoice because you are being used to prevent it from taking place and/or God is using you to make possible a Kingdom advancement in your loved one's life.

Note: This is war. At times there will be intense struggles in the spirit, a give and take, if you will. There will be moments you feel overwhelmed and think that you are not making a difference. Don't give up; stay focused. You have to have strong resolve to persist in prayer. Trust and know that God is at work on your behalf. Persevere!

4. Your Pastor, Leaders and Church

The pressure on pastors and their families is enormous and unprecedented. Due to many factors, pastors face an onslaught of discouragement, self-doubt, and unbridled frustration. In addition, many have to confront dark and debilitating depression. These attacks and others like them lead to burnout, and thus, many good men and women leave the ministry altogether.

One thing is clear: the devil has a ferocious appetite for pastors, their families and church leaders. Since pastors are on the front lines of the battle for the souls of men, they are prime targets for the devil. The enemy knows that when a leader falls or quits, it demoralizes their followers and hinders the cause of Christ in their area.

Please take time each day to pray in the spirit for your pastors and their families. Your prayers could be the very thing that keeps them moving forward, led out of temptation or even from quitting.

Satan knows if he can devastate the leadership of a church or ministry, then the likelihood of a sustainable move of God taking place through their work is unlikely.

Also, pray diligently in the spirit for your church. The enemy loathes the local church because it has been bought by the blood of the Lamb and commissioned to spread the good news of salvation to the entire world.

The agenda of the devil is more than clear. He wants to cripple the Church by influencing believers toward disunity, carnality, and prayerlessness. His goal is to render her completely impotent and ineffective.

Here is how to pray for your local church:

With fervency, pray that the church would rise up

at this late hour and take her rightful place in advancing the cause of Christ.

Pray she awakens from her dreadful slumber. (Romans 13:11)

The Church must once again become a holy example to the rest of the world. Pray she becomes the Bride without spot, wrinkle or blemish (Ephesians 5:26-27).

Pray she would once again be empowered by the Holy Spirit to execute the will of God on the earth.

Pray she would give evidence of the resurrection power of Christ that dwells within her. In other words, that great exploits would be done that magnify the supremacy, as well as, the goodness of Jesus.

Chapter Seventeen

PRAY IN TONGUES NOW

This whole book was written for this moment. You are about to pray in tongues. Prepare yourself to begin to pray like you have never prayed before. Remember, this is God's will for your life. For that reason, you can expect God to do His part, but you must do your part: speak in tongues.

Below is a step-by-step approach to releasing your prayer language.

Hunger and Desire to Speak in Tongues

"Pursue love, and desire spiritual gifts..."
1 Corinthians 14:1

"Since you are zealous for spiritual gifts, let it be

for the edification of the church…"
1 Corinthians 14:12

"Blessed are those who hunger and thirst for righteousness, for they shall be filled."
Matthew 5:6

"Now eagerly desire the greater gifts…"
1 Corinthians 12:31

Ask for it

"Ask and it will be given to you; seek and you will find; knock and the door will be opened to you."
Matthew 7:7

"If a son asks for bread from any father among you, will he give him a stone? Or if he asks for a fish, will he give him a serpent instead of a fish? Or if he asks for an egg, will he offer him a scorpion? If you then, being evil, know how to give good gifts to your children, how much more will your heavenly Father give the Holy Spirit to those who ask Him!"
Luke 11:11-13

RELEASE and Pray from your Spirit - Flip the Switch.

"I will pray with the spirit, and I will also pray with the understanding. I will sing with the spirit, and I

will also sing with the understanding."
1 Corinthians 14:15

Pray this prayer:

Father, I thank You that You desire to baptize me with the Holy Spirit and to give me the ability to pray in tongues. I gladly receive this gift and ability into my life. I know this is your will for me.

By faith, I ask You to baptize me with Your Spirit. Come, now, Holy Spirit, and immerse me in Your power. I receive You now.

At this moment, Father, I receive the gift of tongues that You desire for me to have. Thank You for this supernatural prayer language.

Right now, I will release this language for Your glory! I will speak in tongues.

(**RIGHT NOW - FLIP THE SWITCH** and begin praying from your spirit; use your voice and push out your new language.)

Note: Some of you in the beginning will only express tongues through stammering lips. Do not let that bother you. Keep speaking; don't stop praying and giving voice to your spirit. It won't be long until you will be speaking a clear, heavenly language.

Closing

I am delighted that you are now praying in tongues. Do this every day and as much as you can. But know the enemy will fight you in this area. He will do all within his power to keep you disengaged from this wonderful connection with the Father.

Recognize the struggle and position yourself to press in all the more. Only eternity will reveal the full impact of your praying in the Spirit!

Other Powerful Books and Resources

By Todd Smith:

HE SAT DOWN

This is a must have. It is provocative and revolutionary. For too long, the Church has been waiting for Jesus to do everything. The Bible says, "HE SAT DOWN." God will never do what He has left for His Church/children to do. Todd dares you to read this book. You will never be the same. Will you stand up?

Right now in heaven, Jesus is seated. His work on the earth today has to be done by us. Will you stand up?

www.kingdomready.tv

HE SENT HIM

Pastor Todd Smith, a former Southern Baptist Pastor, removes the doctrinal clutter and biblical misunderstanding to clear the way for you to have a life-changing encounter with the Holy Spirit. He will answer your questions and guide you through every obstacle you have regarding the baptism with the Holy Spirit. This book is a must for those who are searching for the more! Get it for a friend, your small group or for yourself. You will never be the same.
www.kingdomready.tv

40 DAYS - A Journey Toward a Deeper Relationship with Christ

This book is a lot of fun. It is an interactive devotional book designed to help you DEVELOP consistency in your private devotional time.

Most Christians struggle with being consistent in their quiet time with the Lord. This resource will get you in the Word and help develop your faith.

Plus, every new believer should start their new journey with Christ with this book in their hand!

"40 DAYS" is a premier tool that will help you mature in your relationship with Jesus.
www.kingdomready.tv

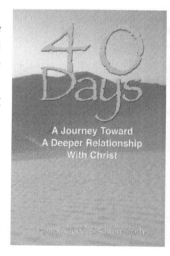

Encounter…WORD POWER!

This is one of everyone's favorites. It is packed with power! Over 360 topical scriptures on such topics as, Leadership, Parenting, Marriage, Temptation, etc.

In addition, over one hundred twenty quotes from various leaders highlight each topic. It's enjoyable and inspirational. And, it makes a great gift for anyone.

www.kingdomready.tv

10 THINGS EVERY PASTOR NEEDS TO KNOW

(Available in digital format only)

I wish someone had told me the truth about pastoring. It has been a joy to lead people, but it also has been difficult. Only one in ten pastors makes it to retirement; ninety percent leave the ministry. This short book will encourage and equip pastors to finish strong.

Get a copy for your pastor!

To Order VISIT US at www.kingdomready.tv

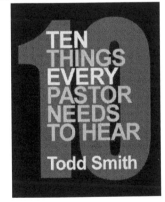

Made in the
USA
Lexington, KY